DUDDESTON AND VAUXHALL GARDENS

Compiled by Valerie A. Preece

Birmingham City Council
Library Services

BIRMINGHAM LIBRARY SERVICES
Central Library, Chamberlain Square,
Birmingham B3 3HQ

1990

ISBN 0 7093 0167 7

FORWARD

When we needed a new piano-back for Vauxhall Gardens School various ideas were considered. I remembered seeing a copy of an old drawing of the Vauxhall Gardens in Duddeston, dating from about 1850, and thought that if it could be traced it would make a good design in needlework.

In the Local Studies department of Birmingham's Central Library I found a small copy of the sketch, which was apparently taken from a painting in the city's Museum and Art Gallery. Thanks to Stephen Price, of the Local History Department there, I was privileged to see the original water colour painting.

This led to a discussion as to where exactly the Gardens had been in relation to the school site. The more information that was uncovered, the more there was to find from other sources. 'Aris's Birmingham Gazette' was a constant source of information as was the Holte Collection.

The research was engrossing; I hope the reader finds it just as interesting.

Maps and prints are reproduced from the collection in the Local Studies Department, Birmingham Central Library.

My grateful thanks to Patrick Baird, of the Local Studies Department, for all the help and encouragement he gave me.

Valerie A. Preece

> The time draws near - another year
> Shall see the work of centuries fall;
> For 'tis decreed - sad news indeed -
> To do away with Old Vauxhall.

So wrote Ned Farmer early in 1850 as he sat in Vauxhall Gardens lamenting the passing of his favourite haunt. The land was to be sold and split up into building plots. Ned and his friends had spent many happy hours in good companionship in the smoke-room, at exhibitions or listening to music there.

The work of centuries indeed, for this was the original home of the Holte family.

DUDDESTON AND THE HOLTES

The name of Vauxhall did not appear until the eighteenth century, but Duddeston is known to be over one thousand years old. A charter, written in Latin, was granted in 963 AD by Eadgar to Wulfget, the thane. Wulfget was probably related to the brother of Wulfruna, from whose name we get Wolverhampton. Part of the charter reads:

> I, Eadgar, King of the Angles, have bestowed a certain parcel of land dispersed in two places, (that is to say three homesteads in the well known place called 'at Duddestone' and three likewise at Aernleye) upon a certain truly faithful thane of mine whom the learned people of this country call by the noble name of Wulfget, in perpetual inheritance for his most devoted service so that having fulfilled his vow, he may possess it throughout his lifetime, with all appurtenances, that is to say, meadows, pastures and woods. **(Aernleye is Arley in Worcestershire).**

The name Duddeston is a Saxon one, Dudda's tun, meaning Dudda's settlement, and there are various spellings of it including Dudestone and Dodestan. What happened to the land, or who owned it during the next two hundred years or so, is not known.

The name Holte is also Saxon, and the earlier bearers of the name are called atte Holte. They may have lived in the area before the Norman Conquest, but the earliest recorded is Henry in the thirteenth century. Hugh, his son, married Maud, a daughter of Sir Henry de Erdington. Maud outlived her husband and is known to have been living in Birmingham in 1327. Her son John, and his son Simon, also lived in Birmingham at that time. Simon purchased the Manor of Nechells (found spelled in a variety of ways - Neachells, Echels, Ochels and Assels).

Simon's son, John, had two sons, John and Walter. It was John atte Holte who purchased, for forty marks, the Manor of Duddeston from John de Grimsarowe (or Grymsawe) in 1365, after the death of his father. His mother was Maud de Grimsarowe, daughter of the man from whom the manor was purchased, and in 1367 she conveyed to John atte Holte, by charter, "the fair Manor of Aston". Thus, Nechells, Duddeston and Aston were now owned by John atte Holte. John had no son to succeed him so Walter, his brother, inherited the estates. In 1400 he held, with the Manor of Aston, four messuages and four carucates of land in Duddeston and Bordesley. A messuage was land with a dwelling house and outbuildings, and a carucate (also called a hide) could vary between sixty and one hundred and eighty acres depending upon the quality of the land.

John, Walter's grandson, held the estates in 1441, followed by his son and grandson, both named William. The younger William's son was Thomas Holte who became a lawyer. He was appointed Chief Justice of Wales and also Commissioner for the Dissolution of Religious Houses by King Henry VIII. This last made him very unpopular with some people as the Commissioners became very wealthy men; with the dissolution, they gave the wealth of the monasteries to the crown, but lined their own pockets at the same time. At the time of his death in 1545 an indication of his wealth can be seen by the inventory taken of his possessions and also gives us an idea of the size of Duddeston Manor itself.

The Inventory of all the goodes and catells, movable and unmovable, plate, juells and housold stuffe of Thomas Holte, Esquier, decessed, made the eigth daie of Apll, in the yere of the reyne of oure moste dradde Souvreign, Lord Henry the Eight, by the Grace of God, Kynge of Englonde, Ffrance, and Irelond, Deffender of the Faythe, and the Churche of Englonde and Irelonde in earthe supreme hedde the XXXVIj th

It goes on to describe thirteen sleeping compartments in the house as

chambur over the buttrie, chappell chambur, the maydes chambur, the great chambur, the inner chambur to the great chambur, the yatehouse chambur, the inner chambur to same, the geston chambur the crosse chambur, the inner chambur to same, the clarks chambur, the yeoman chambur, the hyne's chambur, all the hawle, the plece, the storehowse, the galarye, the Butterye, the ketchyn, the larder howse, the dey howse, the bak howse, the bultynge howse and the yeling howse, also a mylne and aprt of the howse was a chappell.

The principle bedchambers were draped with splendid hangings, those of the great chamber being "of gaye colors blewe and redde"; **one of the beds in the same room being** "wrought with gildinge and fine bise" **with** "a tester of satten blew and redde with cuverleyd of sarsnet **(a soft silk fabric)** of the same collor". **The total value of the contents of this room alone were £13 14s 4d. The complete inventory is on a roll of parchment 15 feet 9 inches long and 5 inches wide and the total value of the contents of Duddeston Manor house is given as £270 6s 2d. The manor house stood on the left bank of the river Rea not far to the west of the present Vauxhall Station.**

Thomas Holte Esquire was succeeded by his eldest son, Edward. The second son was also living at Duddeston in 1579, but whether at the manor house or elsewhere is not known. An entry in the Register of Baptisms of Aston dated 13th September 1579 is for Barnaby, the child of Joseph Holte of Duddeston, Gent.

Edward's son, also Thomas, was born in 1571 and succeeded his father in 1592. It would seen that Thomas was a very ambitious man as he served as Sheriff of the County in 1599 whilst still a young man. He was a member of a deputation to welcome King James I to England and was rewarded in 1603 with a knighthood.

Even then we read of Ulster "being in a state of rebellion" **and King James offered a Baronetcy to every Gentleman with an income of £1,000 or more, a vast sum in those days, whose ancestors had, for at least two generations, bourne arms. The principle requirement was that he should maintain for the defence of Ireland** "and especially for the security of the Province of Ulster ... thirty foot soldiers in the King's army, after the rate of 8d sterling per day". **As this requirement was for three years, the total cost was at least £1,095, and it was for this service that the red hand of**

Ulster was added to the Holte family crest. One year later Sir Thomas
Holte became the first Baronet and began to enclose the land that became
Aston Park.

Visitors to Aston Hall are often told of Sir Thomas killing his cook, but
this event must have occurred at Duddeston. A charge was preferred by Sir
Thomas against William Askerick, "that he did openly, publicly and
maliciously and in the hearing of divers persons, utter with a loud voice,
these false, fictitious, scandelous and approbious words in English,
respecting the said Sir Thomas viz: Sir Thomas Holte took a cleaver, and
hytt his cooke with the same cleever uppon the heade, and clave his heade,
that one syde thereof fell uppon one of his shoulders, and the other syde
on the other shoulder; and this I will veryfie to be trewe". Sir Thomas
lost the case, not because it was proved to be untrue, but because the
court held that Askerick, in the alleged slander, did not swear that the
cook was killed! The time honoured story goes on to explain that Sir
Thomas had boasted to his companions that his cook always served meals
promptly and laid a wager on it. However, unfortunately for the cook, on
that particular day he was not so punctual and Sir Thomas, angry no doubt
at the thought of being made to look a fool before his friends, went into
the kitchen and hit the poor man over the head with the cleaver. Perhaps
someone should have warned the cook how important it was. It was said by
many at the time that it was because of this deed that the bloody hand was
added to his crest.

That Sir Thomas was quick tempered is shown not only in the story of his
cook, but also in stories about two of his own fifteen children. Years
ago, visitors to Aston Hall were shown a small room, where, it was said,
Sir Thomas locked up one of his daughters for several years because she
would not marry the man chosen by her father. The story went on to say that
eventually she went mad and that she managed to escape and drowned herself
in the lake, or mill pool. There appears to be no evidence to corroborate
this but certainly, when his second son Edward married Elizabeth King,
daughter of the Bishop of London, Sir Thomas did not approve of the match.
Edward was never forgiven despite the fact that King Charles I pleaded on
Edward's behalf.

The building of Aston Hall began in 1618 and Sir Thomas moved from
Duddeston Manor to the Hall in 1631, although the work on the house was not
completed until 1635. During the English Civil War, Sir Thomas was a
fierce Royalist and Aston Hall was under siege; it bears the signs of
cannon shot on the staircase to this day. His loyalty to the King cost Sir
Thomas a spell of imprisonment and a heavy fine of about £20,000. Despite
this, he outlived all his sons and died at the age of eighty-three.

Edward Holte was as loyal to the crown as his father and fought at Edgehill
in 1642, being wounded in the battle. He died in August of the following
year of a fever. Robert, his son, succeeded Sir Thomas and Robert's son
Charles, born in 1648, married Ann, daughter of Sir John Clobery. He died
in 1722, but there is a record of a Lady Holte living at Duddeston Manor in
1725. As Ann was still living at that time, presumably the Manor was used
as a Dower House. She died in 1738 at the age of eighty-nine.

The estates remained in the hands of the Holte family. The fifth Baronet,
Sir Lister, ended the succession by direct line for, although he married
three wives, he had no children. In his will the estate went to:

> i) his brother Charles and his male heirs. (Charles had only
>   one child, a daughter, Mary Elizabeth).

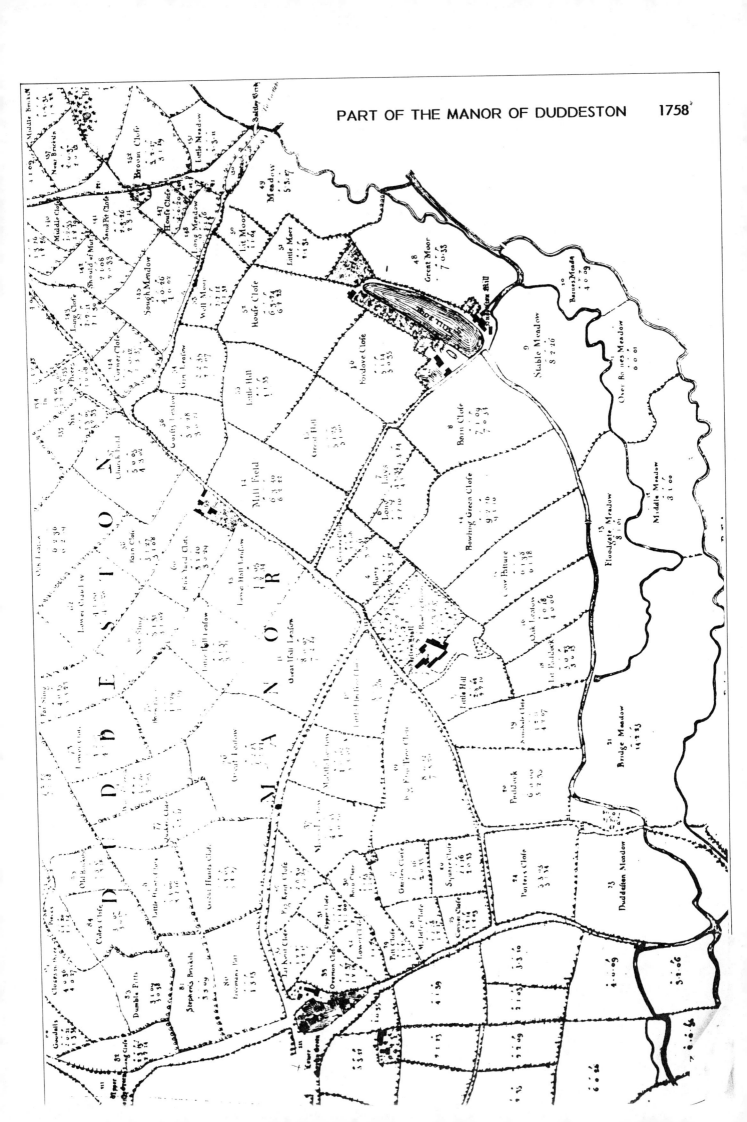

PART OF THE MANOR OF DUDDESTON   1758

ii)   in default to Mr Heneage Legge and heirs

iii)   in default to Mr Lewis Bagot and heirs

iv)   in default to Mr Wriothesley Digby and heirs

v)   in default to heirs general

Heneage Legge and Lewis Bagot were nephews of Sir Lister's first wife. It was inevitable that the baronetcy would cease with the death of Sir Charles but one wonders why Sir Lister worded his will in such a way as to exclude his niece but to allow ANY children of the other three mentioned to inherit. William Hutton made scathing comment on the exclusion "of the infant heiress". Heneage Legge, Lewis Bagot and Wriothesley Digby all died without heirs and the estates would have reverted to Mary Elizabeth eventually. She had married Abraham Bracebridge and he, knowing that the estate would revert to his wife, used it as security. Later when his business failed, he was unable to pay his debts. The creditors wanted their money and so a private Act of Parliament was required to allow the sale and dispersal of the property which was then divided between Heneage Leggge, Wriothesley Digby, Bracebridge and the creditors. And so Duddeston was sold to help pay off debts and passed to new owners after more than five hundred years of Holte ownership.

DUDDESTON MILL

Duddeston Mill and Pool were on the banks of the River Rea. It seems probable that the original mill was built on a different site in about 1530 and the new mill built in 1570. In an agreement made by Edward Holte of Duddeston, there is a reference to "three new cornmills in Duddeston". It was the manorial cornmill in 1741, the lease being held then by Joseph Farmer.

In 1746, Samuel Galton married Mary Farmer, Joseph's daughter. When the lease was taken over by Joseph's son James, Samuel Galton became his partner.

Samuel Galton was of a Quaker family but, because of his trade as a gun-maker, was disowned by his family. Farmer and Galton were merchants and gun-makers in Steelhouse Lane. In 1777, Galton took a lease which gave him control of more land around the mill. On this he built a large mansion called Duddeston or Dudson House, which many years later became used as Saint Anne's School. The mill was used by Galton for polishing and grinding gun-barrels and sword blades.

As the Farmers were ironmongers, it seems likely that it was also used mainly as a rolling mill whilst they held the lease and, in 1756, William Hutton "went with Will Ryland to Nortons at Duddeston Mill to have some silver rolled".

By 1829 it had reverted to being a cornmill, and from 1845 to 1865 the Evans family were tenants. A photograph of the mill at that time can be seen in the book 'Victorian and Edwardian Birmingham from old photographs' by Dorothy McCulla. Shortly after this the mill pool was drained and "the Great Moor", the land between the mill leat and the river, became a railway goods yard. The course of the leat became the course of the river. The mill building was still in use and in 1887-88 was in use as a saw mill. Soon after this the mill fell into disuse.

A LITTLE BIT OF SCANDAL!

On Monday 31st October 1791 a young man and woman arrived at Vauxhall
Gardens. The young man introduced himself as Captain Mouson of the
Dragoons. The young woman was, he said, his sister and she occupied
separate apartments. This was later proved to be untrue. On Wednesday
three men arrived, one of them a Mr Spooner of the Blue Bell Inn,
Leicester. They were in pursuit of Mr Spooner's runaway daughter and, on
his arrival at Vauxhall, he demanded his daughter as she was under age.
The young man refused to give her up and said he would "with his life
defend the possession of her".

The father and his friends returned to the town to enlist the assistance of
Mr Wallis, the constable. The men returned to Vauxhall accompanied by Mr
Wallis, his son and 'Bruce', 'the thief-taker'. In the parlour the young
man had "two brace of pistols on the table and a brace in his pockets". As
Mr Wallis junior started to speak the young man fired. The shot hit Mr
Wallis junior in the mouth breaking six teeth, tearing his tongue and
taking a piece from his upper lip. His father and 'the thief-taker' rushed
into the room and the young man fired again but the pistol misfired and
before the third pistol could be used, Bruce, 'the thief-taker', hit the
young man over the head with his bludgeon. The young man was arrested and
taken back to the town. It was reported of the young Mr Wallis that he
spat out the ball, now mis-shapen and showing "a perfect impression of one
of his corner teeth".

It was believed that the young man's name was Griffin who, under the
assumed name of the Duke of Ormond, had obtained £200 by fraud. A
description of the young man, with the story of the arrest, appeared in
'Aris's Gazette': "He is a most handsome athletic young man, about six and
twenty years of age, is said to speak two or three foreign languages, and
by his conversation he appears to be a man of ability; his whole demeanour
is so very prepossessing and genteel, that many feel themselves interested
in his fate".

It was ascertained that Griffin was wanted in many places for fraud and
deception and was known to have called himself Lord Massey and the Duke of
Ormond. Young Mr Wallis was too ill to appear in court to give evidence,
and Griffin was kept in prison whilst enquiries were made about him. The
young woman was taken home to Leicester by her father.

It was discovered that the man's real name was James Molesworth Hubbard of
Virginia, America. He had duped people in England, France and Ireland. He
had, in fact, been sentenced to transportation in Ireland but had managed
to escape. His mother, an American by birth, had "large possessions in the
province of Virginia" and his father had been the King's Judge Advocate to
the province of Virginia. For these reasons and his charming manner, he
had been readily accepted into the society of the day on arrival in this
country.

At the Spring Assizes in 1792, Wallis was still too ill to attend court and
Hubbard was remanded to the Summer Assizes. When the case did eventually
reach court it took the jury about four hours to find him 'not guilty'.
However, as Hubbard had two further charges against him he was not released
but taken to Suffolk.

On 17th December 1792 the 'Gazette' reported:

On Tuesday (11th December) G. Hubbard, alias H. Griffin, the 'soi-disant'

Duke of Ormandy and Lord Massey, who was lately tried at Warwick for shooting Mr. Wallis, was capitally convicted at the Old Baily for forging and publishing a Bill, purporting to be drawn by Earl Tankerville, for £1,449 and thereby obtaining from Messrs. Green and Willerton, under the assumed name of Lord Massey, jewels and cash for the same. He did not bear his conviction with that fortitude which he before appeared to possess.

On 15th February 1793 a story appeared which told how Hubbard "sent for a Taylor who lives opposite to Newgate, to measure him for a suit of mourning". **The tailor made the suit, which fitted well but, when he broached the subject of payment, the scoundrel replied** "I know that you let out your house at sixpence a head at every hanging-bout: now as I am shortly to be hanged, and you know Mr. Taylor, I am no common rascal, I would advise you to raise your price to half-a-crown. If that wont do, you may have your cloaths again, but I am determined first to be hanged in them".

On the same day appeared: Yesterday morning, soon after eight o'clock Francis Hubbard, alias Griffin, alias Lord Massey and Duke of Ormond, for forgery, and seven other malefactors, were executed opposite the Debtor's door of Newgate. Hubbard stabbed himself in the side on Tuesday morning, and is also said to have taken some poison, neither of which, however, proved effectual; he appeared very weak from loss of blood, but behaved with great fortitude and composure previous to his being executed.

And so, what had begun as a small scandal in Vauxhall Gardens, ended on the gallows at Newgate. One wonders if the girl ever thought of her lucky escape; they never did seem to sort out his christian name!

THE CHURCH OF SAINT JAMES

The church of Saint James the Less, Ashted, was a converted house. Originally the property of Doctor John Ash, it was converted into a chapel when he left Birmingham in 1789. The chapel was opened for divine service in 1791, but was not consecrated until 1810. As it was a privately owned 'Property chapel', the incumbent was a perpetual curate and there was no endowment — the expenses for the upkeep and repair of the building, and also the support of the curate, being met by payment from seatholders. The registers began after the consecration in 1810. Until 1830 there were no free seats but then one hundred and fifty were provided for the poorer inhabitants of the area.

In 1853 a parish was formed out of Aston, and the Ecclesiastical Commissioners provided a series of grants to endow the living; the incumbent was made vicar in 1868. The building was of plain red brick, rectangular in shape with a semi-circular projection on one side. When it was enlarged in 1835 it was extended by half its length again; it then provided eight hundred and fifty free seats. The building was restored in 1887-89 but was badly damaged by bombing during World War II. The ruins were finally demolished in 1956.

Saint James' Church received the first grant of £200 from the National Society in 1828-29 to provide Saint James' Church School. The school expanded in 1869 and a new Infants Department was added in what had been a working men's reading room. Between 1868 and 1870 the school was recognised by Birmingham Education Society and in 1869 the fee was 1d or 2d per week. The school was closed in 1894 because the Birmingham Education

ST JAMES'S CHURCH
ASHTED BIRMINGHAM

Department refused to recognise the school any longer, owing to the condition of the premises which were considered to be in a dangerous state, and the lack of a playground.

Windsor Street Primary School, which was the forerunner of Vauxhall Gardens Primary School, was opened in 1874 and closed when the new school was built during redevelopment in 1963.

THE BIRMINGHAM RIOTS

The year 1791 saw many parts of Birmingham and its surrounding areas affected by riots. Doctor Priestley, the man who discovered oxygen and the composition of water, lived in the town from 1780. He was a non-conformist preacher and was very out-spoken in his views, writing various controversial papers. His scientific experiments were something of a mystery to some of the local people to whom, perhaps, they smacked of necromancy. All this added to misunderstandings which would later erupt. Priestley was a great believer and supporter of liberty and he made known quite clearly his sympathy and favour for the French Revolution. Some thought that because of his views on this he would like to see the establishment in this country overthrown. A dinner held on Thursday 14th July 1791, to celebrate the fall and destruction of the Bastille, provided the final spark to light the keg. A crowd that had gathered outside the hotel where the dinner was held, thought that Doctor Priestley was attending. The angry crowd became a mob and stoned the Old Meeting House. So began the riots which lasted for three days, until the advance guard of Dragoons arrived from Lichfield. The crowd then dispersed but not before many large houses in the town and surrounding districts had been looted and fired, including that of Doctor Priestley.

Another resident of Birmingham at that time was William Hutton who became a well-known historian of Birmingham. Born in 1723, he moved to Birmingham from Derby in 1750. He opened his first small bookshop in Bull Street, paying one shilling per week in rent. Hutton not only sold books but also loaned them out and so began the first public library in the town. Later, he moved to larger premises in High Street and it is from both William Hutton and his daughter Catherine that we can read clear eye-witness accounts of the riots. Their house in Bennetts Hill, Washwood Heath, and the shop in High Street, were looted and fired and they were for a time rendered homeless. During the riots they escaped to Sutton but a feeling of unrest reached there and so they moved on to stay in Tamworth. Once the riots were over, the need to return to a place nearer to their former home brought them to Vauxhall Gardens. It was from here that Miss Hutton wrote to a friend in Enfield telling of their experiences.

The place from whence I date this tells you our home, and a most delightful one it is; but I need not describe it, for I think you have been here. Upon second thoughts, I think you have not, so I will tell you that it is a kind of tavern, with a bowling green, orchestra, woods, and walks, and that during the summer there is a public night once a week, on which there are musical performances, as at your Vauxhall, except that they, as well as the company which frequent them, are upon a smaller scale, and in lower style. Here we board and lodge, that is, my mother and myself, for a guinea and a half the two. Father sups and sleeps here, paying for his supper. We have a spacious dining room, which we are obliged to quit on public nights, when we sit in my mother's bedroom. We choose to eat alone, but do not require a dinner to be provided for us. Upon the whole, we are as comfortably situated as people can expect to be who have lost two good houses.

She then goes on to describe the events in the riots. Mrs Hutton lived
only a further four and a half years but William Hutton lived until
September 1815; he was 92 years old when he died. Both he and his wife are
buried at Aston and Catherine, who was devoted to her father and never
married, lived to be 90 years old and is buried at Saint Margaret's, Ward
End.

THE BARRACKS

The riots began on Thursday evening and much damage had been done, by fire
and looting, by the time the military arrived on Sunday. The first to
arrive were few in number but, as they marched into town, they were greeted
by the more law-abiding citizens and the rioters dispersed. On Monday more
potential rioters arrived from the Black Country but, on the same day, a
larger contingent of light horse arrived to reinforce the original
sixty-four.

When troops were needed in a town it was up to the local publicans to find
lodging for them. This was not always easy or convenient, as accommodation
was not only needed for the men but for their horses as well, which the
landlords thought unfair.

On 17th August 1792 there appeared a report in the "Gazette":
With the liberal view of relieving Publicans of large towns, upon whom a
number of horse and other soldiers are often times very inconveniently
quartered, the Government have adopted the plan of erecting Barracks, where
they will be lodged and provide for themselves. They have already, we
understand, begun to build them at Manchester, Sheffield, and Nottingham,
and last week Colonel De Lancey agreed with Mr. Brooke for four acres of
his land at Ashted, to erect barracks.

In fact the barracks covered some five and a half acres. 28th August, a
little over a year after the riots, saw the laying of the first stone. The
cost was £13,000 and agreement was made for a long lease at a penny a
square yard per annum. William Hutton, who obviously did not approve of
the expenditure, made calculations on the costs and wrote: "... when all
these numbers are added together it will appear that every man's lodging
stands the country in about eleven pence a night, or six shillings and five
pence a week. Half this sum, united to the slender pay of the private
soldier, would recruit the army with men instead of old age and children,
and that without pressing or purchase, the landlord would then welcome the
soldier with a smile, whom he now receives with a frown".

Accommodation was provided for one hundred and sixty-two men and stabling
for their horses, and the centre block was used to accommodate officers.
The work was completed in the summer of 1793. The troops were called from
the barracks for later risings or disturbances in 1792, 1795 and 1799.

In 1797 the Loyal Birmingham Light Horse Volunteers were formed and their
first muster in complete uniform took place in October of that year. By
1798 voluntary contributions from various sources reached over £7,000 and
on 4th June 1798 Colours were presented to the Volunteers.

It seems that the barracks were used as a transit camp rather than a

permanent base for any particular regiment, as there are short comments in 'Aris's Gazette' noting the arrival of various detachments. In 1878 the 11th Hussars were stationed there, followed by a detachment of 5th Dragoon Guards. Two years later, in 1880, a detachment of 17th Lancers were sent to Great Brooke Street Barracks because "the drinking water was considered good for man and beast". In 1889 the 5th Dragoon Guards were there again and were visited by their general. In the later years of the barracks the Territorial Army were making use of the buildings. The caption to a photograph which appeared in 'The Birmingham Post' of Saturday 9th April 1932, records:

Great Brooke Street Barracks, Birmingham, which are to be demolished to make way for a Corporation housing scheme. Occupying some five and a half acres, it is proposed to erect on the site 180 maisonettes. The Barracks have been in military occupation for over a century and have accommodated famous regiments in the past. Latterly they have been used by local units of the Territorial Army but these have now found accommodation elsewhere, the Signallers at Hall Green and the RAMC Field Ambulance at Acocks Green.

The maisonettes were built around courtyards and to some extent resemble barracks themselves. They are now over forty years old and several have been modernised as tenants vacate them and before new tenants move in.

MURDER MOST FOUL!

During World War II the church of Saint James, in Barrack Street, was virtually destroyed by bombing. Later, during the redevelopment of the area, the land was cleared and flattened and some of the remaining gravestones were laid flat and remain there still. Some of them make interesting reading and one in particular tells of a gruesome deed that took place in 1817. It reads:

Sacred
to the memory of the much lamented
Mr. Thomas Pennington
of London, Wine Merchant
Who was most barbarously murdered near this spot
on 6th day of February 1817
Aged 55 years
by whose meloncholy death
an afflicted widow and seven children
are left to mourn the irreparable loss
of a most affectionate husband and indulgent father.
His distressed family derive their greatest consolation
from, the reflection
that the virtues which endeared him to all
who knew him have, after passing this vale
of trouble and sorrow, met with their reward
and that
the affliction which was but a moment hath
worked for him a far more exceeding and
eternal weight of Glory.

Mrs Pennington was, in fact, expecting her eighth child at the time her husband was murdered. A report appeared in the 'Gazette' dated 10th February 1817 giving more details of the victim and the murder:

"Robbery and Murder - We are concerned to state that a most atrocious

robbery and murder was perpetrated during the last week in the immediate
vicinity of this town. About eight o'clock on Thursday evening the body of
a respectable person was found lying in the road between Vauxhall Gardens
and the village of Saltley in a near lifeless state. Upon being removed to
a neighbouring toll-house, it was discovered the unfortunate person had
been robbed, and shot through the head. Medical aid was immediately sent
for, but the unhappy sufferer expired in the course of a few minutes,
without being able to communicate any circumstance attending his melancholy
situation. The body was afterwards carried to Vauxhall when it appeared
that the name of the deceased was Pennington, of the firm of Pennington and
Bellchambers, wine merchants of the Metropolis. Mr. P. left the town soon
after seven o'clock and intended proceeding as far as Castle Bromwich. The
body has since been examined by the faculty and we understand it is
strongly conjectured that Mr. P. was shot while in his gig, and afterwards
dragged to the ground. A ball had passed through the lower part of the
back of the head, and a slug was found lodged within the head. The
villains succeeded in taking from his person a gold watch and some loose
cash, to what amount is not known. The greater portion of the property he
had with him, fortunately escaped their search. The deceased was about
fifty years of age and has left a pregnant widow and seven small children.
The body remains at Vauxhall, where an inquest will be held this day.
Although no actual discovery of the ruffians concerned has yet taken place,
we are informed that our police who have since been on the alert, have
found some clue which, we fervently trust, may lead to a speedy detection
of the murderers. It will be seen that ONE HUNDRED and FIFTY GUINEAS are
offered for their apprehension".

**The rewards referred to were offered in two separate advertisements in the
same issue of the** 'Gazette':

ONE HUNDRED GUINEAS REWARD
Highway Robbery and Murder

Whereas Mr. Pennington, a respectable Wine Merchant of London on the
evening of Thursday late, between the hours of Seven and Eight o'clock, was
stopped in his Gig, between Vauxhall Gardens and the village of Saltley,
near this town, by some villains, by whom he was ROBBED and INHUMANELY
MURDERED.

The above reward of ONE HUNDRED GUINEAS will be given to any person or
persons whose Information shall lead to the Apprehension and Conviction of
the Perpetrators of this barbarous Deed; and should either of the Parties
concerned (expecting the Person by whom the Pistol was fired) impeach his
Accomplice or Accomplices, he will be intitled to the above Reward and
every Exertion will be made to obtain his Pardon.

Any information is requested to be given to WILLIAM PAYN HIGH CONSTABLE OF
BIRMINGHAM.

ROBBERY AND MURDER
FIFTY GUINEAS REWARD

Whereas on Thursday Evening 6th Instant, on the Road leading from
Birmingham to Saltley, some Person or Persons did ROB AND MURDER
Mr. Pennington of London -
We the Churchwardens and Overseers of the Poor of the Parish of Aston (from
a Sense of public Duty) do hereby offer a reward of FIFTY GUINEAS (over and

above any other Reward or Rewards that may be offered) to any Person or Persons who shall give such Information as shall lead to the Apprehension and Conviction of the Perpetrator or Perpetrators of this horrid Deed.

Aston February 9th 1817

The 'Gazette' of the following week gives a short account of the inquest and a verdict of wilful murder against some person or persons unknown. No further progress had been made but, in the 'Gazette' of 24th February, the following report appeared:

MURDER OF MR. PENNINGTON - We regret to say that the perpetrators of this murder are still undiscovered notwithstanding the most unceasing exertions of our police officers. Considerable degree of anxiety was excited on Thursday last by a message received from the Rev. Dr. Wooll, of Rugby, before whom a man of the name of Gardner had voluntarily confessed that he had been concerned in the murder, with two other men of the name of Hiorns. A constable from Brinklow came over to this town for the assistance of Mr. Payn, who accordingly returned with him and apprehended one of the Hiorn's. Upon examination, however, it clearly appeared that Gardner had been inticed to make the confession at the instigation of a man of the name of Fox, in the hope of obtaining the reward offered for the apprehension of the murderers. The innocence of the Hiorns's as to the charge, was most satisfactorily established, as it was fully proved they were twenty six miles from Birmingham at five o'clock in the evening of the day on which the murder was committed. It was further proved that Gardner himself had never been at Birmingham in his life, or nearer to the town than ten miles. He was committed to Warwick upon his own confession where he will remain until the Assizes.

Mr. Payn has received a communication from a Friend of Mr. Pennington, in which it stated that the fold watch taken from the person of the deceased had the name of Ellicott Royal Exchange, engraved on the inside. A purse, which he had with him, is also described as a long green one, with slides, and containing some ? guineas and seven shilling pieces. As no particular account of property taken from Mr. Pennington has before been made public, the above, should any part of if be offered for sale, may happily lead to some clue by which the murders may be detected.

The 'Gazette' of 10th March 1817 then had this report:

The Gazette of Saturday (the London Gazette) contains the promise of his Majesty's pardon and a reward of 150 guineas to any associate in the murder of Mr. Pennington (except the person who actually perpetrated the deed) who shall impeach his accomplice or accomplices so that they may be apprehended and convicted. The like reward is also offered to any person who shall be the means of bringing all or any of the murderers to justice.

Despite all the offers of what were then considerable rewards, it would appear that nobody was ever caught for this murder. There is no record of the rewards ever having been claimed and there is no record in Birmingham of anyone being apprehended. Unfortunately, all the Warwick Assize records prior to 1860 were destroyed by fire and so we have to rely on reports in 'Aris's Gazette' or in the 'Warwick Advertiser' for accounts of hearings and trials at the Assize Court.

The man Gardner, who was held at Warwick until the Easter Assizes, does not appear to have been charged with murder or anything akin to it. In a report of the Assizes in 'Aris's Gazette', Monday 21st April 1817, one Thomas Gardner was sentenced to twelve months imprisonment in the House of Correction for "fraudulently obtaining a silver watch at Rugby". There was no mention of the murder but as he is the only person with the name of Gardner in the lists of either condemned, sentenced to transportation, sentenced to House of Correction, or acquitted, and there is the connection with Rugby, it would seem that he is the same man.

Nothing more is heard of the Pennington affair but the newspapers and public had a far more interesting murder case to follow later that year when Mary Ashford, a pretty young woman, was murdered in Erdington. The events following that case caused a change in the law and was of far more interest to the readers of 'Aris's Gazette'.

THE COMING OF THE RAILWAYS

The coming of the railways was the beginning of the end for Vauxhall Gardens although no doubt at the time no one ever imagined what great transformations of the landscape would take place within a few short years.

Land had been acquired for the Grand Junction Railway in 1835. Work began on the lines from Liverpool to Birmingham and London to Birmingham and the former was completed in 1837. On 3rd July of that year a train carrying a party of directors steamed from Liverpool to Birmingham; the following day the line was formally opened. However, as the imposing Curzon Street Station was not completed in time, a temporary station was built at Vauxhall.

The great excitement engendered by the event can be imagined, as a great crowd began gathering at five o'clock in the morning. The main event of the day was the departure of the first train with a full complement of passengers on their way to Lancashire. Not only was the engine named but each of the carriages as well. An account of the great event appeared in 'Aris's Gazette' of 10th July 1837.

At seven o'clock precisely, the bell rang, and the opening train, drawn by the 'Wildfire' engine, commenced moving. The train consisted of eight carriages, and bearing the following names:- 'The Greyhound', 'The Swallow', 'The Liverpool and Birmingham Mail', 'The Celerity', 'The Umpire', 'The Statesman', and 'The Birmingham and Manchester Mails'. The train started slowly, but, upon emerging from the yard, speedily burst off at a rapid pace. To those who for the first time witnessed such a scene, it was peculiarly exciting, and the immense multitude, as far as the eye could reach, gave expression to their admiration by loud and long-continued huzzas, and the waving of hats and handkerchiefs.

The train travelled at an average speed of 30 mph and even reached 35 mph at times. It consisted of first class carriages only. Another train for second class passengers followed 'at a suitable distance' behind the first, and later in the day a train arrived from Liverpool.

A year later the Birmingham to London line was opened and the railway age had begun for the town. Industry could spread its tentacles more rapidly and with it the grime and soot of many chimneys. The popularity of this new form of transport to Birmingham can be seen in that, during the first

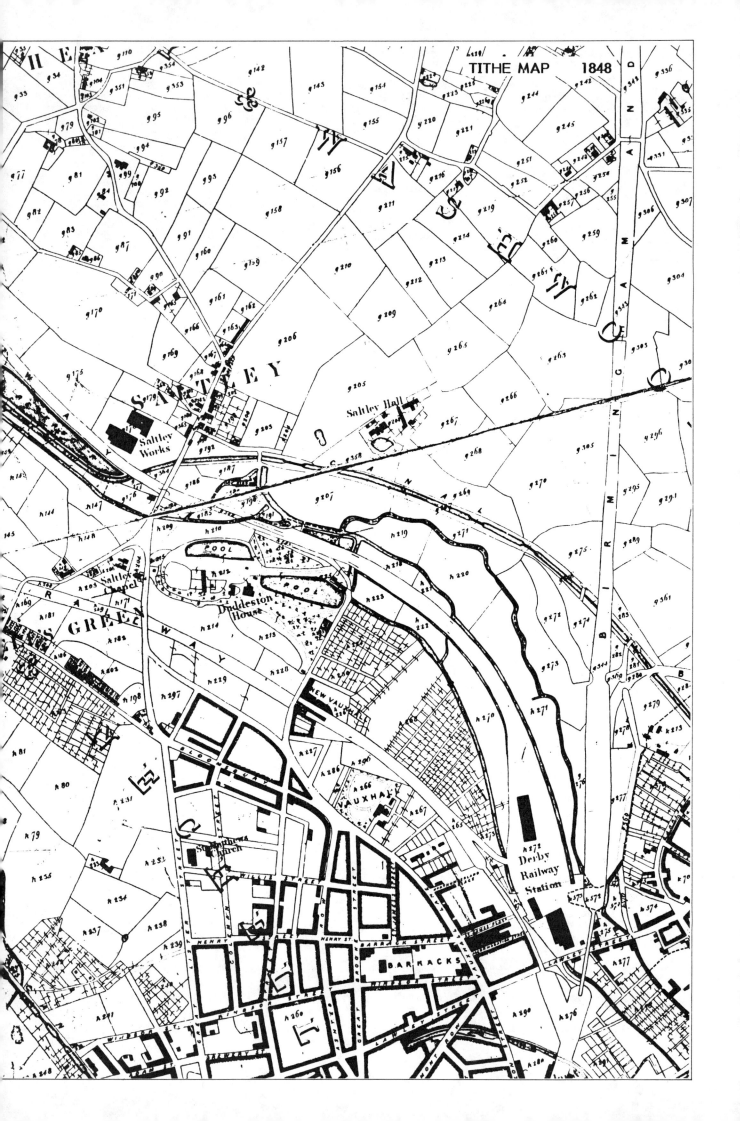

TITHE MAP   1848

nine weeks of the Birmingham line to the north being opened, about eighteen, and a half thousand passengers travelled to or from Liverpool and a further seven and a half thousand to and from Manchester. The receipts for that period came to nearly £42,000, a very considerable sum for that time.

The station at Vauxhall became an intermediate station after Curzon Street was completed and the line was extended; Curzon Street becoming the terminus for both the Liverpool and London lines. A letter to the 'Birmingham Weekly Post' in February 1936, when writing about Vauxhall Gardens, mentions that "the erection of the present passenger station (many readers will recall the old rabbit hutch structure) and the creation of a Carriage siding, carried away the last vestige with the exception of a boundary wall in Dollman Street". The boundary wall can still be seen in Dollman Street, although now very worn and dilapidated, and the station has again been altered and the entrance modernised.

VAUXHALL GARDENS

That the gardens at Vauxhall were extremely popular, there can be no doubt. One poem, 'An Invitation to Vauxhall', was written early in the heyday of their popularity as a place of entertainment and another, part of which has already been quoted earlier, lamenting their passing was written in 1850. As already mentioned, the Dowager Lady Ann Holte is known to have been living at the old manor house in 1725 and it is likely that she did so until her death in 1738. It is not clear who lived there afterwards, but within a few years advertisements began to appear in 'Aris's Gazette' for cock-fighting.

June 1746: This is to give notice - That there will be a Main of Cocks fought at Duddeston Hall, near Birmingham, betwixt the Gentlemen of Warwickshire and Worcestershire for Four Guineas a battle and Forty Guineas the Main to Weigh on Monday, the 9th of June, and fight the following two Days.

In his 'History of Birmingham', Gill writes: "It was the uneducated part of the population, whatever its social rank may be, that mainly promoted the coarser types of sport", but the Holtes could hardly be called uneducated and the prizes were certainly not indicative of a working or even middle class sport. Cock-fighting at that time was considered no more cruel that the Romans considered gladiators fighting to the death or feeding Christians to the lions. It was the 'in' sport of the day and, as in all things, as fashions changed it was realised to be cruel.

1747 saw the next advertisement in the 'Gazette': On Whitsun Monday the 8th June, will be shown at Duddeston Hall, near Birmingham, in Warwickshire, Forty-one Cocks in each Side, for a Match to be fought the three following Days, betwixt the Gentle of Warwickshire, Worcestershire and Shropshire, for Ten Guineas a Battle, and Two Hundred the Odd Battle; and also Twenty-one Cocks on each Side for Bye Battles which Bye Battles are to be fought for Two Guineas each Battle.

It was this battle that inspired another poem which begins:

> Where Dudston's walks with vary'd beauty shine,
> And some are pleased with bowling, some with wine,
> Behold a gen'rous train of Cocks repair,
> To vie for glory in the toils of war;

Each hero burns to conquer or to die:
What might hearts in little bosoms lie!

The poet goes on to describe the birds and the battle at length.

On 28th February 1748 appeared: On Monday, the 11th of April 1748, being Easter Monday, will be a Match of Cocks weigh'd to fight the three following Days at Duddeston Hall near Birmingham, each Party to weigh Forty-one Cocks, for ten Guineas at Battle, and two Hundred the Main; and each Party to weigh Twenty Cocks for Bye Battles for Five Guineas a Battle each Cock to give and take Half an Ounce. The Gentlemen of Worcester and Herefordshire against the Gentlemen of Warwickshire and Staffordshire.

A report on this last match appeared in the 'Gazette' **of 18th April:** On Tuesday, Wednesday and Thursday last was fought at Duddeston Hall, near this Town between the Gentlemen of Worcestershire and Warwickshire, a match of Cocks for ten Guineas at Battle and two Hundred the Main; and the Bye Battles for Five Guineas each. The Battles won on the Main were equal on each side, and the Odds in the Bye Battles were two in favour of the Gentlemen of Warwickshire.

The change of name appears to be gradual and one of the earliest advertisements for Vauxhall Gardens appeared in 'Aris's Gazette' **in June 1758:** Duddeston Hall, commonly called Vauxhall, near Birmingham in Warwickshire, is now fitted up in a neat and commodious manner for the reception of Travellers; it lies in the direct road between Liverpool Warrington, West-Chester, Stratford upon Avon and Oxford; and is much nearer than going through Birmingham. It is conveniently situated for most of the great roads that pass thro' Birmingham, and by going this Way Gentlemen &c avoid riding near two Miles upon the Stones; Hands with Directions will be set up in proper Places; All Noblemen, Gentlemen and others, that please to make use of the House, shall find good accommodations and reasonable Charges, with grateful Acknowledgements, By their modest, Obedient humble Servant, ANDREW BUTLER.
The Garden for Publick Entertainments continued as usual.

Five years later Andrew Butler advertised again (23rd May 1763):

To be Lett, and entered upon immediately, Duddeston Hall commonly called VAUX HALL, near Birmingham in the County of Warwick, being a large commodious House, with necessary Out-Buildings, and a large Bowling-Green: it lies within Half a Mile of Birmingham, and greatly resorted to by the Inhabitants thereof, as well as from other places, being used in the public Way, and in the Summer Season is a concert every other week. There is a Close Cock Pit. The Place is well known to most Travellers. The present Possessor having no Wife or Family has a mind to Retire from Business, therefore any Persons desirous of taking the Place, may apply to Andrew Buttler, of Duddeston Hall aforesaid.

Andrew Butler must have been the first man to lease the Hall and Gardens from Sir Lister Holte. Showell's 'Dictionary of Birmingham' **mentions an old book of 1766 where there is reference to** "near Birmingham there is a seat belonging to Sir Liston Holte Bart, but now let out for a public house (opened June 4 1758), where are gardens etc. with an organ and other music, in imitation of Vauxhall, by which name it goes in the neighbourhood".

FULL CIRCLE

Since beginning the research, Vauxhall Gardens Junior and Infants School

has closed due to falling rolls. The area once taken up by Duddeston Manor and its grounds, which later provided so many homes, had been redeveloped over the last few years. The houses in Dollman Street and Inkerman Street, from where many of the children for the school came in the past, have been completely demolished and have now become Vauxhall Trading Estate. Together with the fall in the birthrate, and the policy of trying not to put families with young children into highrise flats, this has greatly reduced the number of children in the area.

The original cause of this research, the piano-back, will no longer be required when the school closes in July 1981.

With the years Vauxhall grew in popularity and typical of the advertisements and reports that appeared in the press was this of July 14th 1777: At the Musical Entertainments at Vauxhall on Friday last, there was a more numerous and brilliant Company than was ever known at that Place on a like Occasion: The Gardens are in fine Condition, the Beauty of which, added to the elegant Appearance of the Company, particularly the Ladies, the Serenity of the Evening, and the Admirable Performance of the Concert, diffused a Cheerfulness and Approbation over the Countenance of every Person present, highly grateful to the Performers (who seem to vie with each other) and the Proprietor of the Gardens for his unremitting Endeavours to please and oblige the Public.

When Hutton was writing in 1795 he commented upon the growth of the town and its surrounding areas. Of Duddeston he wrote: ... and in 1783 we beheld about eighty houses under the names of Duke Street, Prospect Row and Woodcock Lane. From which time to the present day, May 20th 1793 is the following increase: Belle-Mount (Watery Lane), 26 houses Saint George's Street 5 Lawley Street 73 Windsor Street 63 Henry Street 7 Great Brooke Street 45 Vauxhall Row (the turnpike road) 92 exclusive of a Methodist Meeting House, Barracks for the Military, and Ashted Chapel for Episcopal Worship.

In 1799 a 'Plan of Birmingham' **was drawn that was to appear as the frontispiece to Bisset's** 'Poetic Survey and Magnificent Directory'. **To quote Dent:** In the extreme south eastern corner of the plan are shown the recently erected Barracks and not far beyond it the groves of Vauxhall ... At the end of the century this pleasant retreat with its bright parterres, its numerous gravel walks bordered by lofty trees, its bowling green, orchestra, and other attractions was:-

> 'A rural spot where tradesmen oft repair
> For relaxation, and to breathe fresh air;
> The beauties of the place attractive prove
> To those who quiet and retirement love;
> There, freed from toils and labours of the day
> Mechanics with their wives, or sweethearts, stray;
> Or rosy children, sportive, trip along
> To see rare Fireworks - or to hear a song
> For oft in summer Music's sweet pow'rs
> Woo's thousands to VAUXHALL, to pass their hours'.

Apart from the entertainments mentioned in the above poem, in 1811 a Mr Sadler made a Balloon ascent from the Gardens where hundreds of people gathered, from near and far, to witness the exciting event. In 1823 the same man made another ascent from Birmingham.

'Aris's Gazette' continued to report the happenings at the Gardens and in 1817, several items appeared.

June 2nd : VAUXHALL GARDENS. The proprietor of these Gardens having been disappointed in the intended display of Fire-works on Thursday last, in consequence of the unfavourable state of the weather, intends to have an additional quantity exhibited on Wednesday next; the Birth-day of our venerable Sovereign; when the gardens will be most brilliantly illuminated with various devices in variegated lamps. The Pyrotechnical Amateurs will exert their best abilities in preparing the most splendid pieces ever presented at these gardens; and a band will attend to enliven the scene, by performing several favourite Airs, Etc. The doors will be opened at seven o'clock and tickets 1s 6d each may be had of Mr. Jabet, High Street and at Vauxhall.

June 9th : Vauxhall Gardens. The late refreshing rains have rendered this place of summer amusement most delightful; and the freshness of the verdure and beauty of the foliage are truly engaging. Mr. Steadman is intent on providing amusement of the best description for those who honour him with their patronage this evening, when the most extensive collection of Fire Works ever exhibited will be displayed which with wine and viands of the finest quality will, we trust, ensure a crowded garden.

July 4th - again a display of firework is advertised:
... and the band of the 5th Local Militia will attend and entertain the company with select music ...

August 4th : The birthday of his Royal Highness the Prince Regent will be celebrated with the greatest splendour at these gardens; a most superb display of fireworks by Mr. Moseley will be exhibited; a magnificent Montgolfier Balloon with the descent of an animal by parachute, and a selection of favourite airs, duets &c, by Messrs Horton and Griffiths will add to the harmony and festivity of the evening. We shall endeavour to give further particulars in our next.

The 'Gazette' commented on the growth of the area in an article which appeared on November 23rd 1829:

The rapid manner in which this town has been extended on all sides within the last few years, cannot have escaped the observation of anyone who has recently visited the place. A populous district is now forming between Ashted and the Aston Road, to be called Duddeston Town, and the main Street, named Great Lister Street, has been laid open from Gosta Green to the Saltley, or Halfpenny, Gate, thereby opening a direct road from the centre of the town to Castle Bromwich, Coleshill, etc. Much of this improvement is to be attributed to the prompt and spirited manner, in which the Commissioners under the recently-obtained Duddeston Act have affected the lighting and watching of a district hitherto unprotected and apparently unconnected with the town.

By 1831 house-building was growing fast in Ashted and, although Duddeston Meadows and Vauxhall Gardens remained open, they were beginning to decline. The building of the railway added its contribution to the decline and in Drake's 'The Picture of Birmingham', **1837, he wrote:** "Vauxhall. At the extreme east of the town, eastward, and in the hamlet of Ashted, stand the house and grounds bearing the above appellation - once a favourite resort, but now deserted as unfashionable ... and our artizans and invited to the spot at sundry times during the practical season, to partake of the alluring pastime of "dancing on the green". There is an air of elderly

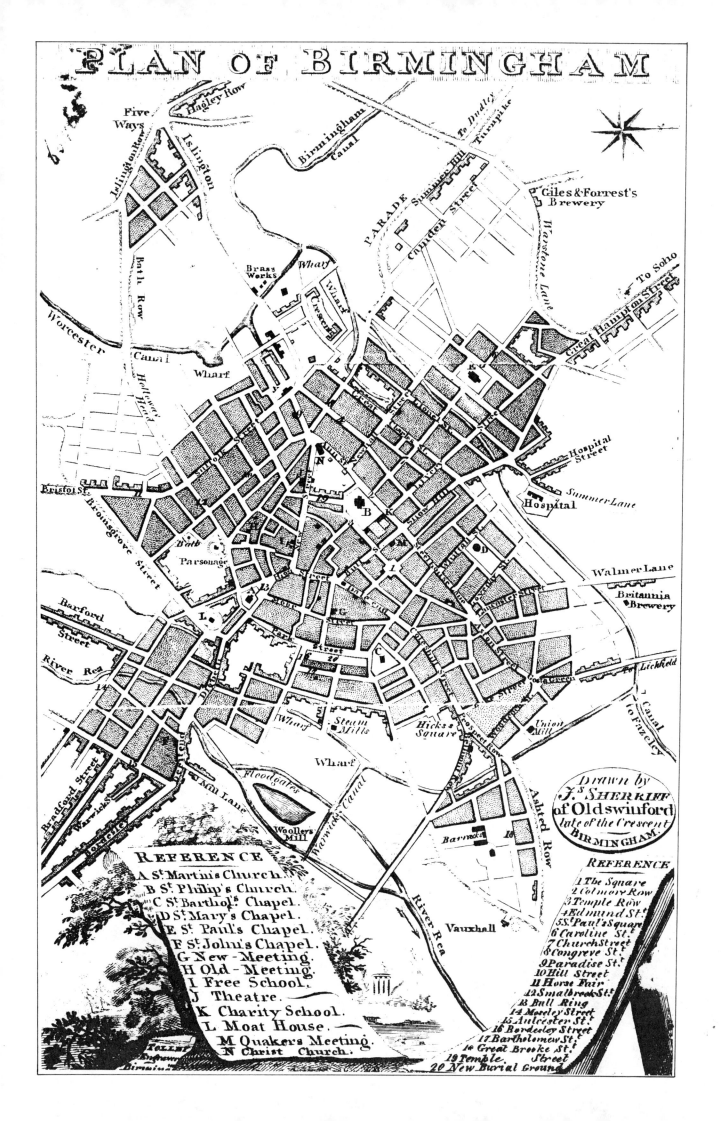

PLAN OF BIRMINGHAM

Five Ways
Hagley Row
Islington Row
Islington
Bath Row
Worcester Canal
Holloway Head
Wharf
Brass Works
Wharf
Crescent
PARADE
Summer Hill
Camden Street
Harstone Lane
To Dudley Turnpike
Giles & Forrest's Brewery
Great Hampton Street
To Soho

Bristol St.
Bromsgrove Street
Bath Parsonage
Hospital Street
Hospital
Summer Lane
Walmer Lane
Britannia Brewery

Barford Street
River Rea
Bradford Street
Warwick St.
Mill Lane
Floodgates
Woollers Mill
Wharf
Steam Mills
Hicks Square
Warwick's Canal
Wharf
Prospect Row
Union Mill
To Lichfield
Canal to Fazeley
Ashted Row

Barracks
Vauxhall
River Rea

Drawn by
J.s SHERRIFF
of Oldswinford
late of the Crescent
BIRMINGHAM.

REFERENCE

A St Martin's Church.
B St Philip's Church.
C St Barthol.s Chapel.
D St Mary's Chapel.
E St Paul's Chapel.
F St John's Chapel.
G New-Meeting.
H Old-Meeting.
I Free School.
J Theatre.
K Charity School.
L Moat House.
M Quaker's Meeting.
N Christ Church.

REFERENCE

1 The Square
2 Colmore Row
3 Temple Row
4 Edmund St.t
5 St Paul's Square
6 Caroline St.t
7 Church Street
8 Congreve St.t
9 Paradise St.t
10 Hill Street
11 Horse Fair
12 Smalbrook St.t
13 Bull Ring
14 Moseley Street
15 Anlcester St.t
16 Bordesley Street
17 Bartholomew St.t
18 Great Brooke St.t
19 Temple Street
20 New Burial Ground

respectability about the place, but without any visible remains of the more, ancient buildings. The situation, until invaded by the approaches of the town, must have been delightful; the grounds, if fashion permitted, are still worthy of notice, being laid out with considerable taste, into lawns and walks, and adorned with some tolerable timber". **It is interesting to note that there was no mention of the ancient buildings; there seems to be no reference anywhere that they were no longer used or that new ones had been built. One wonders, perhaps, if some the old had been renovated externally thereby losing the appearance of medieval buildings. Certainly, the buildings were still called Duddeston Hall at the beginning of their life as a place of entertainment.**

The end was in sight for Vauxhall Gardens, but they were not finished yet. In Longford's 'Century of Birmingham Life', **in 1839 he says:** "Vauxhall Gardens were now in their splendour. Galas were frequently given and singers of first class reputation were engaged", **and to prove his point the following report appeared in the** 'Gazette' **on 23rd September 1839:** "Mr. D'Ernst gave one of his famous galas and in addition to the variegated lamps and the 'magnificent display of fireworks' there appeared Mrs. F. Matthews of the Theatres Royal Covent Garden and Haymarket; Mr. Paul Bedford, the great Bass Singer, from the Theatre Royal, Drury Lane and Vauxhall, London; and Mr. Buckingham, the celebrated Comic Singer of the Royal Vauxhall".

The closing of Vauxhall was a sad occasion for some of her faithful visitors. On 16th September 1850 a farewell dinner was held to mark the closing of the Gardens, followed by a Ball. When the Ball ended at 6am the next morning, the first blow of the axe was struck to the trees.

The land was bought so that rapidly expanding Birmingham could house its growing population. A painting was made before their passing, for the Victoria Building Society, which was displayed in the window of its offices in Union Street for many years. This was the painting referred to in the Forward of this book, from which E. H. New made a drawing. The painting was later purchased by Sir Benjamin Stone.

And so, to quote Dent: "The old manor house of the Holte family passed away". **A small piece of land between the railway line and Dollman Street was still called Vauxhall Gardens right up to the turn of the century but the splendid walks and trees had all gone.**

In the 'Birmingham Weekly Post' **in 1936, letters were exchanged between readers about Vauxhall. One of 26th June 1936, and quoted one 'Robin Goodfellow' who wrote in 1881:** The residents of the district of Duddeston are justly ignorant of the dilapidated state into which that once popular pleasure resort which some may have known as Old Vauxhall, but the great majority as New Vauxhall, has been allowed to lapse. The house itself is in a wretched state of ruin and what is left of the old gardens is desolate beyond description. It is difficult to persuade oneself on contemplating the mournful ruin that this is the last remnant of the famous place wherein the sires of the present generation were wont to recreate themselves and its fine avenue of oaks, its cosy alcoves where Cupid held constant court, its meandering paths and glimpses of sylvan scenery and its famous smoke-room. Forty years ago, there was no resort like it in the Midland Counties. Out of its spacious grounds a number of little streets have been cut and where the fountain stood and emitted its sparkling spray, there is a public house. A Vauxhall gala used to attract the sightseers of the whole town. Here Braham used to sing in the zenith of his great career and here the daring Mr. Green made some of his ballon descents. A goodly company used to meet in the old-fashioned

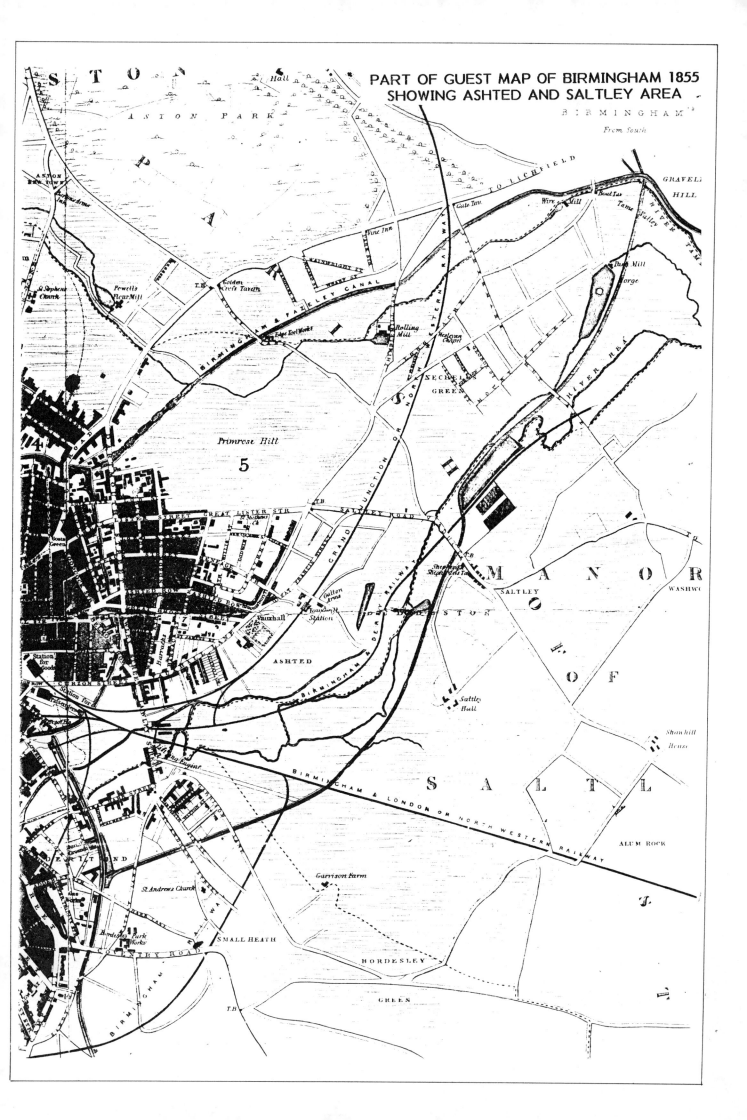

PART OF GUEST MAP OF BIRMINGHAM 1855
SHOWING ASHTED AND SALTLEY AREA

BIRMINGHAM
From South

smoke-room, not the least conspicuous amongst them being Ned Farmer, the
poet, and his boon companion Mr. Charles (afterwards Sarjeant) Wilkins, the
famous lawyer. The proprietor of Old Vauxhall was a most eccentric fellow.
After the old man's death the place went into the hands of his son and more
than thirty years ago the doom of the old gardens was sealed. It was
decreed that they should be cut up into building plots. No one regretted
the change more than poor Ned Farmer.

**On 6th March 1850 Edward Farmer wrote a poem lamenting the passing of
Vauxhall.**

Impromptu

Each passing day doth flich away
Some joy for which it stands our debtor,
And in we range, from change to change,
Not always, mark ye, for the better.
The time draws near - another year
Shall see the work of centuries fall;
For 'tis decreed - sad news indeed -
To do away with Old Vauxhall!

There's scarce a heart that will not start,
No matter what its rank or station,
And heave a sigh when they destroy
This favourite place of recreation.
If we look back on Memory's track,
What joyous scenes we can recall,
Of happy hours in its gay bowers,
And friends we met in Old Vauxhall.

There, fine old trees, the passing breeze
Hath kiss'd for many a long, long year;
This season gone, are every one
Doomed to come down, and disappear!
Beneath their shade fond vows were made,
As e'er "Virginia" heard from "Paul",
For Cupid held an annual court
For years and years in Old Vauxhall.

Enough, enough, 'tis maudlin stuff,
I think I hear my readers say,
Houses are better far than trees,
And Old Vauxhall has had its day.
The pride and pleasure of the town
It long hath been, it now must fall;
Improvement wills it, so prepare
To bid adieu to Old Vauxhall.

Then let the fete, the dance, the song,
Be gayer now than e'er before;
Let young and aged swell the throng,
To view what soon shall be no more.
Let its last season be the best;
One blaze of triumph at its fall;
Let farewell visits be the test
Of what we feel for Old Vauxhall!

It seems a pity that the Gardens had to go and could not have remained as a

park in the midst of the large housing area that, a short time later,
sprang up, but it took a long time for the idea of conservation to catch on '
with planners of towns and cities. The 'improvement' referred to by
Ned Farmer was an area that became built up with hundreds of back to back
houses and courtyards, with few gardens or even trees. These too, have now
been swept away, and modern houses and highrise flats have taken their
place.

VAUXHALL GARDENS

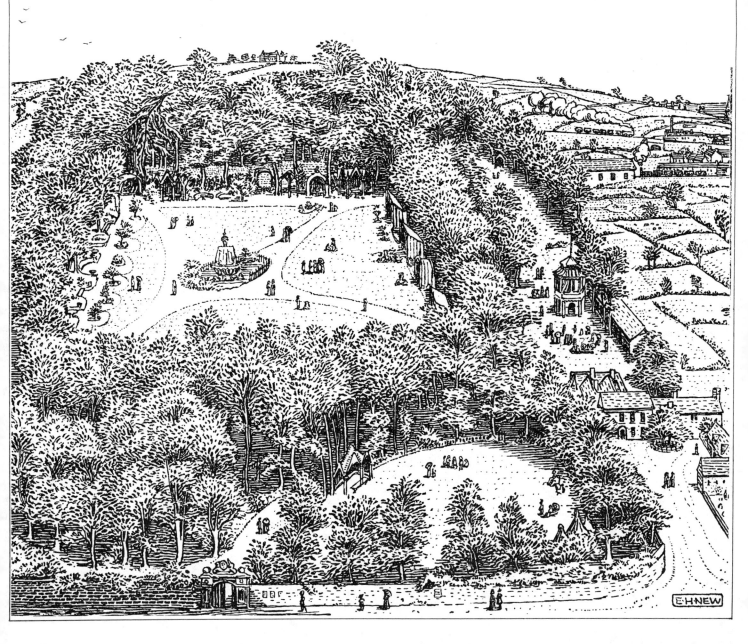

E·H·NEW